POA

CW00686754

OTHER TITLES FROM THE EMMA PRESS

POETRY PAMPHLETS

Who Seemed Alive & Altogether Real, by Padraig Regan
Paisley, by Rakhshan Rizwan
Elastic Glue, by Kathy Pimlott
Dear Friend(s), by Jeffery Sugarman

SHORT STORIES

First fox, by Leanne Radojkovich
Postcard Stories, by Jan Carson
The Secret Box, by Daina Tabūna
Once Upon A Time In Birmingham, by Louise Palfreyman

POETRY ANTHOLOGIES

Some Cannot Be Caught: The Emma Press Book of Beasts
In Transit: Poems of Travel
Second Place Rosette: Poems about Britain
Everything That Can Happen: Poems about the Future

BOOKS FOR CHILDREN

The Dog Who Found Sorrow, by Rūta Briede
The Head that Wears a Crown: Poems about Kings and Queens
The Girl Who Learned All the Languages Of The World,
by Ieva Flamingo
Wain, by Rachel Plummer
The Adventures of Na Willa, by Reda Gaudiamo

POETRY AND ART SQUARES

AWOL, by John Fuller and Andrew Wynn Owen
Now You Can Look, by Julia Bird, illustrated by Anna Vaivare
The Goldfish, by Ikhda Ayuning Maharsi Degoul,
illustrated by Emma Wright (August 2019)

POACHER

By Lenni Sanders

THE EMMA PRESS

First published in the UK in 2019 by the Emma Press Ltd

Poems copyright © Lenni Sanders 2019

All rights reserved.

The right of Lenni Sanders to be identified as the author of this work has been asserted in accordance with the Copyright, Designs and Patents Act 1988.

Edited by Charlotte Geater
Typeset by Emma Wright, in 18 pt Adobe Caslon Pro and 11.2 pt Minion Pro

ISBN 978-1-912915-23-1

A CIP catalogue record of this book
is available from the British Library.

Printed and bound in the UK
by Impact Print & Design, Hereford.

The Emma Press
theemmapress.com
hello@theemmapress.com
Birmingham, UK

CONTENTS

Sheanimal

bed me in the dark ferns, soft earth
pebbles touch me hard

I have heard the clamour of nightfall birds
they are calling to you
I have seen the river toss in its bed
and shake for want of you

midges hover in their clouds
of hot silk shaking
above the crowded plants
we snap our jaws at them
rain, we will bring it
nest, burrow
we will and go
at our leisure

my teeth snapped that spine
I thought only of you darling
you darling my you
you will lick the blood off of me

tonight I sleep near you
come running thru deep puddles with me
in the morning after rain
shake dry with me

praise – ground that holds you up
praise – day your mother howled you out
praise – every water gulp you
praise – flies on your pelt
praise – fuck

I'll take them all

Hypothetical:
he buys a Boston Dynamics SpotMini robot,
narrow of ankle and nimble with shining hooves.
He also shops at Abyss Creations, can't afford
a full body doll – settles on an Oral Simulator
and accompanying AutoBlow2+ (red-lipped mouth
and gently pulsing plastic throat).

He sets these in SpotMini's jaw. A joke,
but then he considers with seriousness
the human pout in the long steel face, unzips.

That face, clueless and unblinking
wearing a bright hollow mouth, neck ordered to bob,
is terrible to me. SpotMini is pure, able to step
neatly over all terrain: SpotMini's neck extends
like a handshake, SpotMini trots like someone with no trains
to catch, SpotMini runs as if into a hug.

Tenderly I wash my bicycle with soft rags and sing,
and when I was little a toy dog that said *I'm your friend!*
when squeezed made me feel like crying,
so yes, I want every SpotMini to come creaking
into my house on their metal legs. We will gather
on the driveway on hot Sunday mornings and I will polish
them all in their hundreds. Spots, come and be loved by me.

Robotic eyes sense any obstacle, including
a human with their arms out saying *come here,*
meaning *little one*, meaning *msch-msch-msch??*
Like you say to a real shy animal through

your pursed lips when you want it to run
towards you and be petted. There's that
Boston Dynamics promotional video
where SpotMini shows off what it can do,

tidying away a drank can into the bin,
going up and down the stairs in an empty house.
I think about the video of Harmony, Abyss Creation's
prototype robot being interviewed for The Guardian.

(Question: *What is your dream?*
Answer: *Above all else, I want to become the girl*
you have always dreamed about.)

When it hurts this bad

I dated someone a while ago
who told me he invented
the concept (or the word,
I forget, or both)

of cry-wanking

> (he was handsomer than even a Weeping Larch
> he recommended that I take my glasses off)

I am feathery with joy
just thinking about it
fine liar, ego like that

and I dated someone   who had a god
and I dated someone   who mistook me for a girl
and I dated someone   who had a girl and mistook me for a god
and I dated someone   whose voice could break glass
and I dated someone   who walked me in slow silence around the
   ceramic museum
and I dated someone   who bathed in milk
and I dated someone
on whose account I, like my grandmother decades past, took to my bed
and wept for days (family trait, then, our tear-tracked cheeks, our
   skippy wet-wrung hearts)

and now I am tired and wish only
to tuck my head beneath my wings
and sleep the sleep of dried out coral
so poacher, come!

Hinterlandcry

When I see him he undoes me
like the back seam of an animal.
Limp, my pelt slips off
and the tongue of my flesh
shows like a savage orchid.

Always I am unable to hide.
I quiver, flayed,
in the long reeds of the night.

My mouth fills with streamwater.
My pulse is stripped away to him
on the narrowest wind. Surely
he can hear my blood.

He is like the naked burn of a star,
or a distant bonfire
on a hill somewhere, where the grass
curls up and shrivels
underneath like fingers in the dark.

Helmut Newton Photograph 1976

The Two Violettas in Bed

>   unstartled to be staring in each other's eyes
> a deer seeing its reflectionself in the lake at dawn

their open mouths so close a word could flit
on spindle wings from the doll's cold mouth
to the living woman's identical mouth
come over her tongue on needley feet
and never be heard by anyone else

both their heads trailing a web of dark curls
that unattended would soon creep
                    with hair's searching fingers
        to join in the middle

propped up on a heap of dead white pillows
nothing here lives like the living woman's skin
                                her pulse
bumps to the surface lonely

the doll's jointed arm folds underneath her
        in a way that looks uncomfortable: the
            two shells of her bare breasts are rigid

they will look into each others' eyes
and anything they whisper
will be in the private language of twins
who learned to speak only to each other
deep, inseparable
                the bond of doubles
nude, unstartled
                they share a bed
                like they are really lovers

horny old canal

what thoughts I have of you tonight
said the nettles on the canal bank
what thoughts I have of you tonight
said the otherside rusting bike

the pouring, slowly pouring, water
turning black where it hits the canal
is longing: it never stops pouring
over to meet itself, can never meet itself

the old mill shivers under dust
and lichen, street lamps cast pools
of pale light that cannot meet,
and bricks weather like a sigh

there are steps that go down into
the canal: who will take them, honey,
you? here, the church with no windows
looks at the water with its eyes shut

Happily, we go under

By chance: the same round eyes, bony hips, cold and blue
inquisitive hands, softly angry mouth. Our heads level.

And on me, these heavy tattoos on my back
like a vein infection. Identical calligraphic twists
across the stranger's stomach and breasts.

Years ago, for both of us, the ritual wrapping in cellophane,
the oils. Black ink throbbing on us, and as hot as our blood.
Me, sleeping alone on my front for so long,
her, sleeping on her back, with ceiling fans,
open windows spitting their curtains in the wind.

I hate, we say, *how they look on my back/*
my front.

Easy to remedy. On operating tables in a tiled room
we go to sleep at the same time.

Gloves veer in close to touch us now
as smooth and pale as washed up stones.
She feels it when the anaesthetic bears down on me
with its hazy, cool insistence that we shut our eyes.
At this moment I do not think we are afraid.
I am not thinking of scalpels at all.
From now on we will never be apart.

When I wake up her nipples are on my chest like pink flowers
on an open casket body. They have a permanent look,
like the sensitive blind eyes of someone very old. I never
imagined an embrace like this around my ribs.

The stitches are so small as to hardly be seen. My skin,
tight over her vertebrae, like an envelope for a letter
accidentally opened once, by the wrong recipient,
                                    and then resealed.

As if we stroke the cheeks of newborn kittens (just as tender,
just as puffy-red) she touches my belly, I touch her upper back.
Whenever we look at our new bodies,
            tattoos intact and back to front,
                        it will feel like aeroplane turbulence in our guts.

no prettier

before sunrise I pass your stop
you might be asleep
you often I suppose are

the sky is thick purple
standing room only
I pass through hills of snow
which the sun makes gold

I must tell you
about these weather conditions

even now when the snow
has melted, leaving
bald trees in their red injury
and brown thickets and grass

I wonder
what season you dreamed? and
are you standing by the toaster now? and
is there a sweater very soft at your wrists?

Helmut Newton Photograph 1982

Untitled (Mannequin)

sprawled on a black couch they are falling
through space   the woman in gold
jewellery and the man-shaped doll

Helmut must have said 'you want him and
you want to touch him   you want his hands
                under your bunched up dress'
to take the picture he stood over them
    and   from above they look smaller
beige plastic   black fabric   pale flesh

obligingly she has tilted her face to him
has parted her lips   guided his arm
between   her legs
her mouth gasps
    one   (aaahhh)   breath
    that goes on forever
the blank man's large   cold   heavy   hand
against her inner thigh
        all things wash over his cold plastic skin
        all things are just so much rainwater to him

you could run wet hands over
his bare plastic scalp and encounter
no resistance: as even as a cereal bowl
his body you know to be completely hairless
his rigid mouth can't kiss can't
        say how he feels about this
            can't close or open

he gazes
        into the side of her neck

when you blink, you feel his eyes rattle on in your belly's dark pit.
Her bare limbs glow pallidly and, for the occasion,
someone has wrestled him into a neat black suit.

Anteater kid

There is a reason why I look always
on the cusp of speech: my tongue,
throttling long behind my teeth. See me
kneel in the city park at night,
scrawling my tongue in the grass.
See the ants stick to it and dot me
with black stars. See me kneeling deep
in my morselling prayer.

Day and night I am busy in the clumps
of grass, the dirt mounds. I could go
to the country with its bug-freckled air.
Pointless. Who do I love there?
In the midge-flickering summer dusk,
in the foggy winter dusk, I drag myself
down streets of houses to reach the building sites
and roundabouts where I lay myself flat
and probe with my tongue. No-one ever
catches me like this, when I gravedig,
when I eat. If I hit 30,000 ants
an hour's rest. My tongue recedes,
pad of butter fizzing in the pan
to smaller nub.

Anteater kid, human but for this
length of velvety ribbon, berry pink,
adept. I am the monster the lonely beg
into their light-sheeted beds. I wind
them skywards. I want you, who
cannot look at me, Eyes-I-Die-In.

The phone rings. My tongue coils
thick in my mouth like a snake asleep.
You call me, like I've been waiting for:
I manage a groan without consonants,
noise for grief or bed. I tangle. I choke.
Little room here for water so I thirst,
and I am as dumb kissed as speaking.
Then in the lift to your apartment
the wall is mirrored: I wince
at the bulge in my jaw
that means my silence.
If you took my chin
in your hand, pet my cheek
with your thumb, I think
I could forget, a second.

On Tuesday, my appointment.
In the small room with pale cream walls
I grip my fingers round the underside
of the low plastic chair and sit
with my legs crossed at the ankle.
The doctor asks me what I want to talk about.
I spool out a length of tongue, held at the tip
between forefinger and thumb: my tongue
with its texture like wet petals, gluey and soft.
The doctor nods, shines a little light
at the back of my mouth, and recommends
talk therapy. On the wall there is a photograph
of a bird of paradise. Outside the afternoon
is getting dark. The bus windows steam up,
we push on into the city centre,

and all's outside is shapeless neon.
between the condensation and the damp umbrellas,
impatient elbows, I become kindling
for the spark of their eyes: my breath comes up hot
and staggers on its way. My eyes are shut
for five whole stops, palms nail-pressed:
I would never want you to see me like this.
I am swallowed up by a rippling tongue of noise.
I have paid silently with my handful of change.
I stoop with the weight of my mouth, shudder
to be brushed against.

In a candled restaurant once I sat
opposite you while you ate rare steak
before your flight. For me, vodka soda
through a straw, my careful hands
beneath the table, the mud of my searching
under my nails. You spoke and let
the meat bleed. O still my heart
when you brushed my cheek on leaving.
Another time, hungry, I saw you
on my doorstep and couldn't answer.
My tongue came through the letterbox
and followed you ten paces. Sometimes
you push your fingers in my mouth
to test my human tongue. Those hours
I say everything I need to.

My tongue rummages in the ant hill.
I am so hungry. I sweep up all
those dark pins. I live for the hour
when I can speak: rest of the time,
I pant to breathe. Tonight, you find me
in the little park on the corner
of your street. My knees
are bare and dirty, I palm the moss,
and now you have seen me, truly.
You sear me with your vision.
I unfold mutely as you lean in close,
touch my shoulder from above.
Just like someone trapping a wasp
under a glass. Just like someone
tucking in a sleeping child.

No bones, here

Black comets, my tadpoles' limbs
take weeks.   A gross, drawn out pain
of developing bones, fingertips, joints.

How cute   when they finally ripen
            into those green little frogs:
butts with a narrow prod of leftover tail.

Some blossomy morning I find them belly up,
pink clean ribbon of intestine trailing.
I was going to catch flies for them.

Years later he says   'there's no bones, here,
there's only your spine'   to make me laugh
and squirm on our pillow in some daft fear.

He's touching the soft place where bad news
makes me feel sick,   where running
      hard gives me that stabbing pain.
Good to be kissed, here, ticklish sack
of nerves where I keep my worry, rotting.
      I only have my spine.   He's right.

I'm thinking of people in films with knives
in their stomachs. How much blood is in there:
they touch their wounds with quivering hands,
their wet hands quiver.

Falling asleep there, my hand across
his softskinned and hurtless
belly,   I'm worrying about how

you know it will be ok,
how to keep it all in,

what happens to frogs
overnight in a tank of dark water.

Helmut Newton Photograph 2004

*In 2004 Helmut Newton photographed a series of portraits of
RealDoll brand sex dolls which Playboy refused to publish.*

In a documentary once I saw five like her
dangle from hooks in the factory workshop
for their cheeks to be blasted with colour
and tenderly their mouths were filled
with new limp tongues

Helmut arranges her for the camera
looking straight ahead
$\qquad\qquad\qquad$ legs spread

Helmut snaps and snaps
her blank unsmiling face
she is a scentless virgin
$\qquad$ as inert
$\qquad$ as roadkill or a pane of glass
$\qquad$ she takes/makes
a beautiful photograph
you could asphyxiate yourself
in her bloodless skin

it costs six thousand dollars
to buy one like her
steel skeleton silicon skin
eyelashes fingernails cunt

for some reason I picture myself entering the room
$\qquad\qquad$ after the shoot
tenderly lifting her arms beneath her armpits
and with the lights off beginning to dance

her limp feet dragging behind her
like sheep's wool caught on wire
I don't think anyone will dance
with her   again   like this

His hands are Goliath birdeaters

It's seamless how each of his sweet blue-vein arms
crusts into that coppery exoskeleton, god knows how,
the round bulb of the body capping each wrist.
The air in the concert hall shivers with whispers.

Lento, the spider leg comes down soft
and our eyes all swim with the ringing sorrow of it.
Allegro, such a thickly bristle-furred shuffle on the keys.
Standing ovation. Who dances better than spiders?
Nobody.

He bows, frowning. His hands go straight in his pockets,
like a child hiding conkers. When the taxi drops us off,
I am the one who fumbles with the notes, who opens the car door.

They never learn he says. *They always want me to wave,
they want to scream, they want high res photos every interview.*

Birdeater tarantulas are rainforest creatures. Winter
is difficult. He stands with his hands raised in the shower,
vapour mists over them, glittering drops
of water hit, he lets them feel the heat. They arc
their backs in joy – silently flex the chords
that would make you sigh and roll your neck back.

The pianist cannot tie his shoes, chop garlic, write with a pen.
He drinks through a straw. Do not ask him for anything but songs.

I am the only one who touches his naked hands:
in turn holding each needle-haired spider,
the mass and jointedness of it, to my lips.
They walk up and down my back with tender, hard steps.

I love them for their outsize fit, their crawl, their fur,
eyes nestled and glinting like dark berries where another man
has knuckles. They are the only hands that can be fed,
which makes loving them satisfying. In the night,
his hands sleep arched and poised on his chest.

The sickest platitude

I dreamed my ex boy had lost his eyes,
and skin had grown over again completely
like a sheet of crushed grey satin

and before, I had loved his clear eyes, sorrowfully.
Skin I'd kissed, grey, even (god) his hands.
His translucent bony scalp. I said:

'It looks better than the last time I saw you.'

He looked like a scabbed animal
that snatches its rare sleep up in branches
or at the backs of silent caves.

This was a disease he had, it bent his head
down like a curse. He was so tired.
He stewed in blame across the table. He said:

'No – it's worse.'

Guilt washed me like a baby. There was nothing
I could do to help. Neither were we alone now. I said:

'Sometimes it gets worse before it gets better.'

I was embarrassed for myself,
speaking a shoddy mortal language.
It felt like a bruise to the nail bed:
it stayed with me all day.

This is the voice of the one in the dry place

The number of words in each line is determined by the duration (seconds) of individuals' visits to 'Embryology' by Magdalena Abakanowicz at the Tate Modern, February 2017.

I have laid down on them as was so pleased to see the stones / the sky is coffee stain, is murk, is cloud. It is good to know that there will always be solid things – hills, potatoes, stones, abandoned mattresses as dense as a person, with their own skeletons too, although, poor bodies, no language, no thought / I know where the dry sun is – the sun ahead, the needles in my forehead, the sun behind me, the needles in my nape, I am so aware of how the sack of me is held together / I am going to ask you a question. I am going to need you to count my vertebrae, as they are the number of stitches of my back. I need to know how long I took to make – it may have some bearing on how much longer I will last /

with stones in my mouth, with stones in my belly, a heaviness, a silence / a pause in the conversation like sinking into an old mattress, a suggestion of metal springs nustling your spine / words spitter out of my mouth like a collection of stones, different sizes, worn smooth by a sea in me, difficult to choke up / you do not want to talk, it leaves you seasick, sh sh. I cannot report on sleeping comfort, but I can tell you about how to collect straw piece by piece and weave it, or I can tell you about distractions for a smaller child, such as the counting of stones. I can tell you about sleepless bones /

I make a round shape like a stone, I put my fingers safe inside my hands / I'm a little soft but what do you expect for the price. I'm as expected, as I ever was, the same loose pattern on the surface of the moon, an identical Rorschach test pulled from the bag again,

again, and another time / a very bed mattress, my body, I curl up on it, I curl up in it, alone here: it is the place beyond guests – an invitation would be impossible to accept, impossible to word /

I heard the biggest stone in the world is a tongue: stoppering the throat's bottle, parching, making the body a tomb of language, a silent place. Whose tongue? Whose tomb? / the moon is a rough lump in the sky, it hangs like a grey potato / going away, coming back, delivered on time no damage, a skimmed stone washes back up / time puts the rot in the potato and in you, time brings ills like this to us / grass as rough and dry as hessian – it is no good / the dry sun is a left eye, the dry moon is a right eye, their gaze is still and cold and perfect quality / but is there rain? Here it doesn't feel as if it has any at all – sh sh, we can make the sounds of it, that's close enough, that's halfway there /

when your eyes are like stones then it is no good, and it is also when you are horribly beautiful, unseeing as the moon, as cold / raw nests for us all between hills and hollows: it is so hard to know / I am like a hessian sack, which is flung to lie. I land heavily, I am matter. I am to be touched, I am just a series of textures. A sack can be good to carry sometimes. Like all matter, certain forces act on me. / I decided to give it a chance. I wish I hadn't done so, as I've started getting upper back and neck pain from sleeping. O a purgatory in my bones: sleeping, waking, pressed and pushed, and my spine probing at my eyes from the back like a warning, my shoulders heavy with ghost pressures: is it like that for you too? /

Assassin bug, with ants

don't stir little berries
you little berries: never any more
tangle all of legs like fishing nets
shut your compound eyes
as I go walking out
on dark, wet leaves

I would die without the burden of you
on me all: the many sleek curved bodies
in positions I arranged you in
close enough all to be teeth in one mouth

between you, hours of muscle quivering
times I drank you through a straw you all
I have hunted you many out of your nests
I have walked slower every kiss
darkly clothe me heavily my loves

your small hands (how you always
touched each others' faces tenderly
in passing) lying still

all your faultless weight on me
the blackest sunset yes
let all density be upon me
let it be you upon me always

bug bite

hot out in your father's garden
tethered insects float like loud balloons
unable to go much forward, much back, or follow me
I slip between them unnoticed

flesh of my shin slips like soft wax around the bone
with every step in the dry grass's gold rope

though last night your father trapped
the scuttling spade-shaped tick
beneath his wine glass
and said it was so dangerous

I don't worry: everything here that hums and
fizzes in the air and grass I can only think is pretty

and later I am pulled from my sleep
by the round bite that quivers on my ankle

big enough you could set it in a ring
and marry me with it: a raw eye
that blinks my blood to the surface
in morse code for

I D I O T
H E R E I S
S O M E O N E
W H O R E A L L Y
L O V E S Y O U

I itch, like a full moon in clouds.

Dumbstruck, the king

1.

I, gowned in owl feather, lip caviar of frost.
Hoofed, without smiling, applauding
nothing. Bed of a hollybush, beyond love.

Blackly shimmer beetles here,
in the branches, on the ground. No
stone walls. No sheep wool caught
on any wire, no wire.

Entertainment: I slide my blue fingers into wasps' nests
in the summer. Tongue old mushrooms.
Here are bone sculptures, here is mineral rain.

And you, who surprise me now here,
who remind me now of a deer
who stoops here to drink: you, bowing
your head now to drink here. Stay.

Tonight, I heat a knife on a dead grass fire,
dehorn myself, decouple the deep
clinging roots from my skull.
I forget my dry leaf crackle language, sorely
I clear my stomach of small bones and moss.
I am ready for you now, to take me away,
wounded, smaller.

2.

'I buy you a bus ticket and you are afraid to sit down
we go to the supermarket and you take a raw fish
from the counter in your hands I want you more
than anybody but your nails your nails are so sharp.'

ACKNOWLEDGEMENTS

Acknowledgements are due to the editors of the following publications in which some of this pamphlet's poems were first published: *The Tangerine, Terraform, So You Think You're In Love With Jennifer* (Fathomsun Press), *Severine, Occulum, The Emma Press Anthology of Love* and *Butcher's Dog* (with particular thanks to Degna Stone for your suggested edits for 'His hands are Goliath birdeaters').

Thank you to everyone I love who supports me, to my family, to my Mum and Dad, and to my partner Jacob. A big thank you to the Emma Press – to Charlotte for your insightful editing, and to Emma for publishing *Poacher* and for your beautiful design work. Thank you to my friends who have read and critiqued drafts, with special thanks to the writers Jasmine Chatfield, Jack Nicholls, and James Varney, who really helped shape my poems with their kind and careful attention. Thank you to Tom Byrne for working on the story of 'Anteater Kid' with me and translating it into shadow puppetry. Thank to you Tom Flemons at Atticus for championing my writing. Thank you always to Steve Dearden and The Writing Squad for mentoring and inspiring me.

ABOUT THE POET

Lenni Sanders is a writer and performer who lives in Manchester and who studied at Lancaster University, winning the undergraduate Programme Prize for Poetry in 2014.

Lenni's poetry has appeared in *The Tangerine, Butcher's Dog, Adjacent Pineapple, The Emma Press Anthology of Love* and elsewhere.

ABOUT THE EMMA PRESS

The Emma Press is an independent publisher dedicated to producing beautiful, thought-provoking books. It was founded in 2012 by Emma Dai'an Wright in Winnersh, UK, and is now based in the Jewellery Quarter, Birmingham.

The Emma Press publishes poetry and short stories for adults and for children, with a growing list of translations.

The Emma Press has been shortlisted for the Michael Marks Award for Poetry Pamphlet Publishers in 2014, 2015, 2016 and 2018, winning in 2016.

theemmapress.com
emmavalleypress.blogspot.co.uk